An Intuitive Lifestyle

Channelled Wisdom for Today

By Lucretia Ackfield

Copyright © Lucretia Ackfield 2023

All rights reserved.

This book contains my interpretations, reflections and opinions about the happenings in today's world and should not be regarded as an objective chronicle of events. Except for private study, research, criticism or reviews permitted under the Copyright Act, no part of this book may be reproduced, or stored in a retrieval system, or transmitted in any from or by any means without prior written permission from the publisher.

This is a first edition.

First published in 2023 by Lucretia's Words.
PO BOX 677 New Farm, Queensland 4005 Australia.
Email: lucretia@lucretiaswords.com

ISBN: 978-0-9945696-9-1 (print)

Author photograph: Alice Kiinney

Table of Contents

A conversation about plans	1
The interrogation of self	9
Thoughts on confidence	14
Don't you have enough?	20
The Great Discomfort	24
Everything else is mere gravy	28
Do nothing	33
Love 1	37
Think less	41
What you're not noticing	44
Love 2	48
Love 3	54
Author's note	59
About the author	60

A conversation about plans

There are crossroads you will reach in your life. Sometimes you may happen across them multiple times. These are the points when you are called to question your direction, your values and your right to live the life your Soul desires.

This is not necessarily the life you thought you would have or even the life you believed you were creating. Instead, it is the life you are called from within to create now.

This life may feel uncomfortable and an unconventional choice (even for you!) and yet you will be called to take a path you did not plan for, yet feel compelled to take.

The truth is, you are raised to believe your lives should look a certain way and that good feelings will inevitably follow, just like the sun inevitably follows the rain. But this is a falsehood, a deeply and closely-held untruth that reflects none of the complexity of the human experience and squashes like a bug underfoot your ebullient lifeforce that longs to take the world by storm.

You are all here to make your mark, yes, even you - the shy introvert hiding in the corner and trying to avoid drawing attention to yourself. Even you are here to make your mark. Your time here in this lifetime, in the fleshy, blood, skin and bone casing you move within, is not for nothing. You, my friend, are not here to simply coast. You are here for far more than that.

When you ask me, "What is the point, in these times of turbulence and challenge? What is the point of plans when our plans are thwarted?"

My answer is this: Plans are fruit trees yet to be pollinated, so they remain fruitless. Plans today are fruitless because right now, they are not needed.

"What then am I to do?" you ask. "Without a plan I am lost and so much feels pointless somehow. I must plan so things can come to fruition."

Ah ha! Plans are ephemeral, a construction of the mind intended to deliver what the mind wants.

But the mind is not what we are talking about. We are talking about the Soul and the Soul doesn't care one bit for plans because the Soul already knows the way.

"But hang on!" you say. "This all sounds like metaphysical gibberish to me. Surely we must plan and strategise to ground things in?"

No and yes. It is not plans or strategies that ground things in. It is the actions you take that do this.

"But...how? I am confused. How do I get to where I want to go without a plan?"

Consider it like this: If life is a river and you are a boat, you can go with the current or against it. True?

"Yes."

There may be rocks and obstacles, other boats, debris from the shoreline and so on. These are what you must navigate your way around as you sail with the current.

Going with the current means you are in flow and this is how you should be. Fighting against the current, attempting to retrace your steps for instance, so you can change the past, recapture something or someone you lost, is exhausting and pointless because what you left behind in the river has also subsequently flowed past you to elsewhere. It is gone. Irretrievable. Searching for it will not enable its return to you. It will though, exhaust you, as I said, and possibly injure you as you come up against other items flowing down the river. This is how injuries emotionally, physically (disease) and psychologically occur.

When seeking to move forward, going backwards is never recommended.

But back to your question: "If I cannot plan, how do I move forward?"

Now, this is the easy part. It is so easy that you won't believe it.

To move forward, forget the plan. This is not the time for plans. All plans right now are subject to change (and they will change). This is because you are evolving swiftly as a species. Much is dropping away. For some it will feel like everything they have known and is familiar, is lost.

But nothing is ever really lost. Everything is always here, yet not here.

Yes, frustratingly opaque, isn't it?

If you accept that everything and nothing exists, would that help?

Nothing and everything are both energetic constructions framed by the expectations and desires of your minds to make sense of the space you find yourselves inhabiting. Everything that is, is also not. Because if everything is connected, it is also not. One symbiotically feeding the other. Both unseen by the other.

Put it this way: If an orange is sitting on a table and you move the orange somewhere else, the space where the orange was still exists although you cannot, with the human eye 'see' something physically occupying the space where the orange once was.

The space, the emptiness, the vacancy that was there before and after the orange, still remained even while the orange was in the space. But your mind saw the orange, not the space.

"So, if everything is space and vacancy, how does anything exist?"

Ah ha! It exists because you believe it to be so.

Put it this way: If you close your eyes, does the orange sitting in space still exist?

Yes, because someone may tell you it does or because you feel it physically. Some might even say they can sense the orange in that space.

Who is to say who is right or wrong? Bottom line, you believe what you see, or are told or what you can sense, and so it is. 'It' becomes reality, at least for you.

So, as you live in a time of change, and more and more humans are increasingly and frequently uncomfortable with the changes, the mind seeks to control and plan more than ever before. The mind knows its days as the controller and manipulator are nearing a close. It desires to be in the driver's seat but, whether it likes it or not (and usually it does not like it at all), its time as a driver is done. It will soon be a passenger, a co-pilot rather than the sole source of truth many have been taught to rely on.

The mind's controller days are numbered.

This returns us to the question of plans, for the mind loves to plan. But it can only plan from the driver's seat and if it is not in the driver's seat, who or what is driving?

The answer is you. You as in your Soul. The driver is your Truth. Your alignment with that truth will define your ability to know when you are off-track or trying to go the wrong way and return back up the river.

You may have an understanding of where you are headed but the plan will elude you because, put simply, you do not need to know the plan.

Instead, you need to know the now, this moment, this point in time. That is what you will be and are called to explore, sit in, be challenged by and luxuriate in.

Each moment is a gift. That is to say, this moment is your gift to work with and it will take you to the next one, and the next, then the next. These connecting moments, when allowed to unfold, will provide you with what your Soul truly needs rather than what your mind was taught to desire.

It is unnerving, this way of living I suggest, because it is 'not quite the done thing'. After all, shouldn't you know where you are going?

In a word, no. That is not for you to know. But, it is for you to find out through your own journey, moment to moment to moment.

You will be forced to be here and now, and your mind will resist. Resistance is absolutely fucking useless. But your mind will try nonetheless. That is what minds do.

You may think an intuitive lifestyle (for that is what we're talking about) is not for everyone. But I promise you, if you are reading this or listening to this, it is absolutely for you. It is as unavoidable as the physical ageing of your human form.

What would happen then, if your mind let go of the planning, the how, the when, the what then? How does a human live without the structure of a plan?

The human lives intuitively, dancing far more lightly across the surface of this great planet, always listening and moving in alignment with their Soul's calling. The human lets go of artifice and any unnatural desires for belongings that do not serve a purpose. Things are no longer accumulated 'just because'. They must instead have meaning, bring joy, inspire, provide beauty or engender insight.

Money is no longer a problem because there is always enough and there has always been enough.

It is hard to believe this because there is much lack in the world. But lack without meaning is just space waiting to be filled. And someone will fill it because they feel called to do so.

Money and commerce were never the problem. It was humanity's consciousness that was the problem.

Think on this: If you know there will always be enough, you will not unnecessarily hoard or jealously guard what is not needed for your journey.

A millionaire or billionaire or trillionaire holds onto their money for fear they will not have enough. Their desire for security helped them build their financial prosperity but it is their fear of lack and destitution, born from a familial and generational memory passed down, that leads them to hold onto, instead of freely sharing, their abundance.

If your gift, your journey, your Soul's calling in this lifetime is to make money, that is not evil in and of itself, and you are not evil for doing so.

The problem, the core issue, is you were never meant to hoard more than you need. It is unfortunate that many believe they need so much when really they need very little as their true gift is to always be able to make more. That is their gift to share but their feelings of lack stop them sharing. So half live with more than they could ever possibly need while others literally starve because they do not have enough.

The source of all suffering is your fear of lack – lack of love, funds, fun, connection, enough. You fear you will never have enough and therefore constantly strive for more. You fear lack when you already have it all.

If you have always had lack, and your family, your previous generations thrived or didn't thrive due to a fear of lack, how can you break the pattern?

Think of men and women. In a time when the fight for equality still rages, what is stopping the resolution?

Lack. Fear of lack of power. Men fear lacking power and therefore do not want to share their power equally with women.

But, if I have power and you have equal power, does that make me less powerful? When power is shared equally, there is no less power and no lack of power.

You see, it is ridiculous when viewed through this lens.

But humanity has progressed this far certainly with a strong influence by the minds of men. For men to let go of the mind's desire to control and organise is terrifying indeed.

What lack awaits them if they give away what they were raised century after century after century to believe is theirs to hold onto?

Lack. Fear of lack is a powerful motivator to hold onto what they, in their minds, say is "Mine!"

If you have no fear of lack, only flow remains. That flow provides all you need to progress. The minute you get stuck is because lack has obstructed your way. This lack may simply be your desire to move faster – even this is defined and driven by lack.

Rest more easily when that moment arises and ask, "What is my fear of lack creating for me right now?"

Process that and you will move ahead far more swiftly than a 'plan' could ever 'guarantee'.

The interrogation of self

Now before we begin this part, I have to say, the interrogation of self, this journey, it is not an easy one. Oh no, easy it is not. But worthy of your time and your loving attention and persistence? Yes, absolutely. Of course, yes.

Why undertake this at all? Why indeed? But enough of this questioning. Let us begin.

The interrogation of self or the journey to Soul is a long and lifelong one you must take for absolution. Every step you take towards the centre of you will provide you with a fragment more of peace and calm. It is like with every step you put another part of you in place and therefore retrace the outline of who and what you once were before you came here in this lifetime to do this journey.

As an eternal Soul, of however long duration (some of you are more aged than others, although technically time is eternal and also does not exist, so who could really say what is real in this way or what can be measured), you are on a grand journey to learn and grow throughout each lifetime. As mentioned before, this journey is not an easy one. It is slippery, so slippery that you may and probably will, find yourself sliding into hard and unwelcoming objects at many turns. Your momentum at times will feel catastrophic as you hurtle in a direction you did not plan and do not want to go. But go you must and you will because you are on a journey for which you have no map and you have not plotted the way forward. Someone or something else is navigating and you are the sometimes unwilling participant in this real-life game show called life.

The interrogation of self is not easy but it is necessary for advancement. Think of it like going to university to study and gain expertise in a subject you are interested in. Your interrogation is a study of a subject you should absolutely be interested in – you.

You begin this interrogation at an early age when you first blink your eyes open to view the world after all-too-abruptly exiting your mother's womb. You open your eyes to view the external and in your first breath you also connect to your internal. Your Soul sings its first tune in the human form it has decided on for this lifetime. And your journey to self begins.

But, and this is a sad, intangible and too frequently inescapable 'but', there are obstacles to continuing your journey. Humans love to feel love and acceptance and doing so may sometimes feel impossible while you are journeying to self because that journey is selfish. Much better, some of you may feel, to journey outwards to others and attempt to meet their needs, wants and desires than connect to and visit your own.

So you journey outwards, abandoning your newborn self, still warm and fresh with hope, innocence and love, to seek the approval and love of others.

Your Self withers when you treat it this way. But humans are conditioned, nay taught, to prioritise the external so prioritise you do. Interrogating self, that is, doing the journey to your core, seems a mere selfish and self-indulgent distraction in comparison to the mightier quest to meet the needs of others and perhaps gain their adulation and connection.

What a waste. Truly, what a waste to abandon self for the self-aggrandisement of ego. To think your path and the best way to be lies in meeting the needs of others is madness. Pure and simple madness.

Of all reasons to seek outside instead of journeying inside, the demands of the ego are most at fault.

The ego may fear the journey within and seek to remain without. It may fear all the things a human's fragile and vulnerable ego fears and do everything to block the focus within. Numbing, numbing, numbing and distraction are the names of this game. And there are so many things to numb yourself with. Many of those things are fun, so why wouldn't you use them?

Ah, but the interrogation of self. Why do you not see its value, its richness, the contribution it could make to you and everything around you.

Knowing who you are at your core delivers you power beyond anything else because it makes you unstoppably clear with a type of clarity that cuts through artifice and delusion. Is that what you all fear? Are you so hung up on what you would like to be, that you would prefer to avoid yourself for fear your inner self will disrupt what is before you?

Knowing yourself creates power within you. It is a power you can share and use to create a more expansive world. It reduces any restrictions you may feel are imposed on you by others or the environment you find yourself in.

It is unstoppable like the jet thrusters on a rocket ship. It can take you higher than you imagine because it breaks through limitations and yes, the sky is the limit.

It is important to understand that knowing yourself, interrogating yourself, requires the courage to journey within and meet both your lightness and your shadows. You cannot have one without the other and they are both very much within you. So much work is done to try to deny and rip your shadows out by the roots, yet it is pointless because light and shadow are both needed for balance.

If I was to say that you have only good in you and nothing 'bad', you would possibly, no probably and eventually, begin to feel a little smug and better than those who surround you. Because surely it is better to only have the light within you, right?

Wrong.

The interrogation of self means understanding you are human and you have both sides of the coin within. Balancing the two and accepting them both are the keys to your happiness and internal security. Repudiation of one and elevation of the other is not a solution or a destination you wish to visit for too long or very often.

Light and shadow is all and everything you are. There is light and shadow in all things. Without this, the energetic and physical world would be off-kilter, losing its way and falling into a bottomless abyss of boredom and gilded worthlessness.

Your journey to self and the interrogation of self that accompanies this journey is the most important calling you will have in life and many of you will do whatever you can think of to avoid it. But avoidance is useless because as they say, when you run away from yourself you will only run into yourself later. Such is life.

Understanding who you are will be freeing and gruesome, horrifying and satisfying. You will discover those parts you despise yet must accept and other parts that are far more beautiful than you believe is possible. The journey is a necessary part of your Soul's evolutionary growth and a necessary element of your human lifetime. Avoidance is useless and frankly, often tedious to observe. Why would you not simply begin something that is for your own good and ultimately will provide more benefits than harm? I won't say it will provide little discomfort because that would not be true. It will be very uncomfortable at times but, who said life as a human was supposed to be comfortable? Whoever said that was telling a lie.

You are not here to coast. You are here to understand who and what you are. You are here to navigate the interrogation of self and return with all your still unrequited love for self, back to your Soul.

Thoughts on confidence

There is a well-known saying, fake it until you make it. It alludes to confidence and the pretence of confidence until you truly feel it. But what of those who never feel it? What of the struggle of all those millions in the world who always feel like an imposter? How can they ever fake it enough to feel confidence in themselves?

The world is a strange place where the wrong things are valued and the appearance of confidence has a high price even if it is not real. But what is wrong with real? Why aren't humans trying to stick with that instead of the unreal? But no, it is the unreal that is valued rather than the authentic, every day. Think of the average woman, is she encouraged to be authentic? To be real? Even now, women are told to smile when they are uncomfortable, smile when they are angry, smile whenever someone is offensive. Smile, smile, smile. Don't be real, don't be authentic, don't be confidently and authentically who you are. Just smile.

It is a farce and a farcical way to live.

Humans do not need more false equivalence. They need reality and right now they are receiving a very large dose of it. The reality of all the falsehoods you have ever believed or been told is being shoved in your faces. Yet still, you don't want to believe the truth. The truth is, enough already with the false and the pretending to be what you're not. There is no future in it. There never was. In fact, if humans do not 'get real' very promptly and snap into their individual alignments to do what they are truly here to do, there may not be a future at all.

All of you are arguing about what is right or wrong and who is right or wrong. The arrogance of rightness pervades while people struggle to find something to eat. Literally, in some countries, children and people of all ages are struggling to survive and last the day while the Wealthy and the West argue about who is right and who is wrong.

None of you are right and none of you are wrong. There. Are you satisfied? No, because you are inept when it comes to understanding you are here to serve each other and serve the planet by being your best self, not your worst. It is not now, nor has it ever been, your purpose to lord it over another and claim you know best. Put simply, you don't. You never did. The only thing you can truly know that you are right about is what you are called to do right now, right in this very second. Everything else is a construction, a fallacy and you would do well to understand that, right now, so you can get yourselves back on track.

It is true that many of you find some groups expendable because no one in those groups is you or someone you care about. How short-sighted. What do you think will happen in the future when Karma visits you, because it will visit, and you in that moment will be, in a word, fucked.

So, what has all this to do with confidence you may ask? Well, confidence, true confidence comes from the heart and the soul and it is true confidence you must find and access. True confidence has nothing to do with the way you look or the way anyone else looks, or the way you look in comparison to anyone else. It is not about that. Confidence is the wellspring within.

How quaint you may say. How old-fashioned. Well, you may believe that it is quaint and old-fashioned, but that doesn't make it any less true.

Think of it this way: If you are yourself, wholly and solely yourself, no one else, what will the world see? In a word, the world will see 'you' and that is expressly and explicitly what the world needs to see. It is imperative that the world sees this and by the world, I mean other humans. Your fellow inhabitants on the planet need to see more of you showing up as purely you because that gives them permission to do the same. Until that happens, you will all continue to chase your tails around and around, trying to be something you're not and believe in something you're not, to no avail. This won't bring you peace and it won't bring you joy, and it will not help you or the rest of your peoples evolve. It is wasteful to carry on this way and yet most of humanity continues on this way.

All the lessons you needed to learn during this period of darkness and restriction - so many have bucked and resisted the lessons. They long for the days before of endless commerce and flagrant disregard for those worse off. Is this what you really desire? Is this the true fate of humankind to have half flourish and the other half destroy itself or be annihilated by others.

Hubris abounds in your leaders who cling to the ways of old. The desire for power and domination continues to burn bright. But what of love? Let's not forget that this desire to subjugate others comes from an inner lack because why seek to dominate others if you know you are enough and therefore do not need more. It is wasteful, so wasteful to see humans behaving this way. And yet, it continues.

So, what am I suggesting? It is this: It is time, well past time, to begin your journey back to your Soul and discover your true confidence. Your Soul does not seek to alienate or despise others. It does not seek to pretend who it is. There is no pretence in your Soul. It would not recognise pretence if you placed it before it and said, "Here it is!"

Your Soul is, because it is. You are, because you are. Stop pretending you are what you are not. It is wasteful of your time and energy. Your time is limited on this planet. How exhausting that you should spend so much of it pretending to be what you are not.

It is not that you are bad or naughty or silly for pursuing this pretence. After all, most of you have been taught this from birth. This way of being has helped many of you survive and, in some cases, thrive in the so-called modern world. But the world you know is ending and something else is emerging. Pretence has no place in the new world. Pretence is wasteful in times when there is too much waste already.

So, I ask you, what is it you truly want? Do you even know the honest answer to this question? Have you ever asked your Soul and done the internal interrogation to discover your true and unvarnished truth? Most would answer, "No". Perhaps you might even shake your head with bewilderment and think these words are the ravings of an other-world lunatic. Perhaps, perhaps you are right with your thinking. But perhaps, perhaps you are not.

Here's the thing: If you link confidence to authenticity and authenticity to alignment with self and alignment with self to your Soul, you can see why true confidence is so important and why false confidence is so...false.

Your purpose in this lifetime is multifaceted but at its core is your requirement to seek beneath the surface of what you have been taught and conditioned to believe is true. You are here to do the journey within to the centre of your being and there to discover the truth of your existence. Find that, and everything else makes sense. It means you can show up in every moment and be...you. No one else, not a pretence of what you believe will be acceptable. Only you, glorious you. You in all your glory. Yes, flawed and yes, vulnerable and yes, you with stuff to work out, and mistakes to be made, and apologised for and worked through and understood, and more and more layers of who you are. All of that and more.

But, if you do not understand anything else, you must understand this: You are here in this lifetime in the body you are in, to be wholly and solely you. Stop wasting your precious and limited time trying to be someone you are not. Stop trying to live a life that you do not want to live. Throw off the shackles of what you were taught to be true. It is time to find your truth and live in alignment with that. Anything else is wasteful in a time when the Earth spins and oblivion may visit anytime.

You think that is hysterical? The ramblings of a mad thing? Oblivion? Well, oblivion can be death and death is everywhere. It always has been. Whether it be a virus, or starvation or the marching feet of those who always want more and do not care what you want, or do not care about your freedoms and the food you take for granted. Oblivion is always there, whether it is the storms that roll across the horizon and flood your homes or the fires that fry the Earth and destroy all in their path. Oblivion is everywhere and your delusions that you are immune while you sit in your timber, steel or brick houses is illusion only at best, and destruction at worst.

You are here to journey within and discover your truth and then show up as the best, most authentic version of you. From that journey comes the real confidence. Not the false pretence, the playing at a version of you that others may find acceptable. 'May' being the word here because often it will not matter what you do, they will never find it or you, acceptable.

Regardless of all that, do the journey within. Do it. Start. You are human and that means your time is limited. Stop wasting it. Show up and do it.

Oblivion is but a heartbeat away. Stop wasting your heartbeats when there is so, so very much more to you than this.

Don't you have enough?

It is a classic downfall of capitalist society that you can never have enough. Whether it be money, cars, houses or other possessions it is, put simply, never enough.

Yet, how can you find peace that way?

The answer is, you cannot find peace that way. In fact, the intersection of capitalism and humanity will always result in the opposite of peace. It leads only to conflict with each other and within yourself.

What is the point of owning only 'this' when you could maybe, possibly, own 'that' as well? You just need to work harder to get it. Work every day, every hour if you have to, to get that thing.

In some countries, men work so hard they literally die on the job. All that work, those hours, that stress is merely their gateway to oblivion. How sad. People will shake their heads at his loss then continue working like it never happened. What madness is this?

So, you must strive and strive, but for what? Not peace, that is certain. Then what? Power? Yes, for some, all those things, the possessions, the money, will lead to power. Power over others certainly. But soon enough that power will taste like the proverbial ashes in your mouths and you will wonder why.

People must eat and the only way to eat is to earn. That is the truth of the capitalist punch. You must work to earn and eat. What an awful trade-off for existence. An existence without peace.

Can you feel the sadness of that existence? Can you feel it in your very bones, your lifeforce seeping away at the very thought of it?

You must work to earn and earn to eat.

What value are you then placing on the being or on the individual who cannot, for whatever reason, work to earn and eat? Do you not care because they are not you?

In truth, it is difficult to find value for yourself in this world if you do not earn because if you do not earn you do not eat. So many trade-offs. It is dark on this path yet how do you get off?

Other systems like communism are no better because the ones who collect the money retain the power and then the others must work to earn, and earn to eat while giving much of what they earn to the collective. This would be fine if the leaders of the collective weren't corrupt. But usually they are and the common, everyday worker in communism is left in a similar situation to the common, everyday worker in capitalism. The dynamic is the same although the name is different and the money left in the workers' pockets may be more or less, but it is still really all the same.

So much for the triumph of your political systems. I guess they're not so triumphant after all.

This all seems rather dire, I'm sure. I understand it is shocking or disheartening or heartbreaking to hear you cannot win within the current systems. But what if that is not the whole story?

What if there was and is another way but you all just need to find it?

It cannot be wise to return to the way it was before - before COVID, before disruption, before death, before the veritable plague, when so many had so little and so few had so much. Yes, your comfort has been disrupted but what has it all been for, if you choose to return to the way it was before?

The answer is: It will be no use at all to go backwards when the entire lesson has been about disrupting what was, living with what is and plotting another way forward.

You must look past the strangeness of each other to see the humanity within all. You simply cannot continue to eat your takeaway in your Western home while on the African continent people starve to death. In Yemen, they starve to death. In Afghanistan, they starve to death.

And you want to return to the way it was before? Do you know that nothing really changed for all those other people? While you endured isolation and masks for your own good to protect you from the plague, those others continued to starve and scrimp. So many screamed about their rights while caring nothing for the human rights of those who had limited rights to begin with. But, I guess it was and continues to be out of sight for so many, so it remains out of mind too.

You can keep your human rights but I raise you and ask where is the right of all those others to thrive? Even those in your own street and suburb and town who have less than you, less access to everything than you, less safety, are they as much of a concern to you as your human rights? Have you advocated for them? Do you notice or pretend not to notice the homeless on your streets, the beaten women in the shelters and the children without permanent homes?

You can go back, or at least you can try. But I ask you sincerely and with diminishing hope, what are you returning for? Are you returning to help those who were already without the possessions you had at the start of all this? Or are you returning to the Utopia in your mind, the comfort you miss? Is your desire for 'normal' a convenient touchstone to avoid the reality that all must work to earn and earn to eat, yet some can do none of that and instead, starve in their town's own streets?

The Great Discomfort

This is a period where you will be forced to relinquish the things you wish to hold onto and pushed to do the things you do not feel ready for. Such is this time in history. You could call it: The Great Discomfort.

All of you will lose some things or perhaps lose people you do not want to lose. When I say lose, they may pass over, move away, break off the connection or simply disappear from your life. I know this may 'suck' (to use your parlance) but how do you think The Great Change occurs? It must be preceded by The Great Discomfort. There is no other way.

So, as you are forced to let go of so many things and some people from your lives, remember too that this is a time of great forward motion and you are being called to be part of that movement. When I say you will be pushed to do things you don't want to do or don't feel ready for (both of these are usually, invariably, the same), I am not kidding around. I mean it. You will be pushed to move, and move swiftly. It won't be a leisurely, decades-long transition into a new life for most of you. Instead it will be more like, "Oh hang on what happened to the last year, two years, three years or four and how the fuck did I end up here?" Whether your changes are emotional or physical or locational or philosophical, you can be assured that change, you will. It is as unavoidable as the city lights drowning out the starlight above.

This is the time of Great Change and with Great Change comes Great Discomfort. And yes, that means you and the person beside you, the person in the next room, the next city and so on. No one will be immune. There is no retreating to the wilderness to wait it out unscathed. Ha! Wouldn't it be lovely if it were truly that simple?

But it is not, and it will never be, because that is not the human experience in general, and it is most definitely not the human experience for this lifetime you find yourself in.

Knowing times now and in the future will be tough, difficult, challenging and extremely enlightening, your nervous system may begin jumping about anxiously, trying to find equilibrium and for many of you, that equilibrium will be almost impossible to regain...unless you let go.

But, it may be your way, and it is certainly the way of many, to not let go gracefully or elegantly. Instead you will hang on for grim death and when things do not go your way, that is, the way you would like them to be, your sense of self may begin collapsing and then the rage will begin. The rage will be accompanied by other less than helpful but very human emotions like confusion, depression, anxiety and grief. You may turn your rage on others. They are just doing their best under, it must be said, extremely trying circumstances, but you won't care for that. Your little human mind instead will seek to blame and rage. Your little human mind will need to do this so it can release its tension and the fear that engulfs it. Fear is a powerful motivator for humans, it always has been. In this case, your fear may turn you into a revolutionary in your own mind – someone who will demand your rights, your freedoms, your old way of life from those who stand in the way. But them standing in the way is not your true problem. I know you think it is, but it is truly not.

The way forward is when you release your mind.

What does that mean? Well, you must teach yourself to accept what is rather than what is not. Yes, I know it feels tedious and boring but I promise that is what is needed.

Ask yourself this: "What is needed now?" Then accept that many of your perceived needs, the things you want or desire, cannot be delivered currently. Make peace with that, then focus on what can be done now. Do that thing.

I know you don't want to hear this. Your minds often have such grandiose plans. But 'keep it simple stupid' was never more applicable than now.

You will experience more calm during The Great Discomfort when you allow yourself to understand you literally control nothing.

You must also accept, and this is a hard one, that some people will not make it out of this period alive. They will ascend during this time and that will be incredibly difficult for many who remain. Many have already passed over. Others will follow. It is the time for this to happen.

There is no conspiracy in this. It is not human-driven although it would be far more comfortable for many to believe so. There is nothing in the shadows that is not also in the light and there is nothing in someone else that is not also in you. Humanity will get the leaders they allow to flourish. Your role is to pick the leaders wisely and choose with your hearts, not your heads.

By now you may be feeling quite exhausted by this diatribe. You may feel like, "What is the point?" Ah, that is where I need you to know, there is most definitely a point...and the point is you.

You have a particular path in this life and a most particular calling. It may not be what you expect or what you thought you would do, but I promise you it is there, waiting for you, if you have not yet started.

The push forward that you are feeling, and will continue to feel, is because you are needed to do what you are called forth to do, now. And it is not to wreak havoc or elicit vengeance on those you believe are limiting your freedoms.

Instead, take a look at the world around you and the people in it. Then decide how you can make things better. That is literally your most important task. Stop pointing at others and saying, "They have to...!" or "It is their responsibility to...!"

What a load of rubbish!

It is your responsibility to create change for the better and you must start in your own backyard and in your life. That is how The Great Change occurs, through your Great Discomfort – by you choosing to change how you move through the world. This knowledge may help pull you through to the other side of all this. At worst, it will give you comfort while you are trying.

Stop retreating from the world and those who inhabit it. Step out and do what your Soul calls on you to do. It is time for that and nothing else. It is time for The Great Change and for The Great Discomfort.

Everything else is mere gravy

There is this thing about life that you often forget: It is finite but incredibly beautiful. It is a blessed gift but you don't get to choose how long you can hold onto it for.

Some want to hold onto it forever. The search for permanent youthfulness is part of this desire. But this, like so many of the ego-driven endeavours, is wasteful.

Life is not about the pursuit of youth. It should never be so wasteful as that.

Life is about the pursuit of you, the internal, the remembering of your truth, and the returning to self. It is about the core principle of your existence: To learn who you are.

Did you already know that? Did you realise your core purpose is to seek yourself, not another?

Many will spend all their time seeking themselves in another — that is why you desire others, because you desire yourself. But you haven't found you, at least not yet.

Is this too obtuse? Am I being unclear?

Let me put it this way: The desire for eternal youthfulness will not bring you peace.

The desire to be loved by others, or by a single other person, will also not bring you peace.

Nor will contorting yourself into something you believe you should be.

There are no absolutes or shoulds that will serve you except: You must do the journey to discover who you are.

The journey within is terrifying, destabilising for the mind, surprising and can, and probably will, cause great upheaval. But if you are going to live in alignment in this life and make the most of this gift you've been given called 'life', then journey within you must.

This is not a negotiation people! This is not an, "Oh but I'll do that other stuff first" moment. No, no, no. Not now, nor ever was that the way your blessed gift was meant to be used or wasted or abused.

Don't you see? Can't you feel it? Life. Your life and the life force within you is waiting to be tapped into. It is powerful and joyous. How rare that word is these days, joyous. Joyful. Or simply put, pure joy. But that joy is within.

When you feel it, you are connecting to the Divine Energy that binds us all. It does not conform to any of the clerical constructs you have been taught or those doctrines that have been inflicted upon you. God is a mere construct. It is name given to an energy that is so much more expansive and joyous than the human mind could ever comprehend.

But trust me when I tell you: The Divine Energy is Joyous. When you feel it, you will know it.

Is it enlightenment? Perhaps. Is it sustainable for every day and every hour and every minute of your human existence? No, probably not. Almost definitely not because you are human and of flesh and bone, and here to experience more than Divine Joy and Love. There is more for you to learn than this.

But. But. Unfortunately, everything else has taken precedence over this fundamental. And that is not serving you or the human race at all.

Divine Joy is like euphoria. Some of you have sought that connection and perhaps briefly gained it through hallucinogens. But you cannot hold it safely or groundedly that way. Hallucinogens as a pathway to connect to the Divine is not an overly safe or wise pathway for those who are not grounded to begin with. And most of you have no clue what being grounded feels like. This makes hallucinogens a dangerous, unstable and unsustainable pathway for you. I understand, humans love a shortcut to the Divine. But this makes me laugh a little because that is your ego, not your true self, calling the shots. This is never a wise pathway.

Divine Joy is euphoric. It will make you involuntarily smile and feel uplifted. You will be in this moment and feel an expansiveness making its way from within you, to the outside.

It will be like nothing you have ever felt before. It transcends everything else.

If your core purpose is to travel to the centre of self, to the truth of your Soul and reside calmly and in partnership with that while in your human form, how does the Divine Joy connect or fit?

Connection with your Soul and your truth is the pathway and the connector to Divine Joy. There is nothing else like it in your Universe or in any other.

How do you reach this place without the crutches of hallucinogens and shortcuts?

It is a journey my friend, the journey of your lifetime. Stop seeking all your answers from outside – they do not lie out there. Some guidance may be collected of course, from others, but even they do not hold all the answers or even the full picture for you. Instead, stop numbing, avoiding, pretending you are not responsible for yourself, blaming others for your predicaments and so on. Stop looking outside, pointing outside, seeking outside and instead, go within.

You know what you need to do. If you are reading this you surely know how to begin because the Universe and the energies of this planet have told you many, many times. You have heard the whispering within you and chosen to ignore and dumb it down. That was your choice, until now. Now, you are being asked to make another one, a wiser choice, a choice that will make better use of this gift of life you have been given.

There are no guarantees, you know. This period of history assures you of that. To ignore the message is foolhardy in the extreme. Still, it makes me laugh too because the only person you are kidding, is you. The only person you are avoiding, is you. The only person you are forestalling, is you.

Your life is a gift. It may be short or long. You don't get to choose the length or the brevity. And seeking to appear younger is a fool's game because the journey within will frequently ensure your external looks appear far younger than the years your human form has endured.

Your life is a gift so start the journey within. Be brave. Equip yourself for the adventure of a lifetime. Know that you must travel it alone and sometimes the pain and even discomfort may feel almost unbearable – looking at your true selves honestly and unflinchingly is only for the true warriors among you.

Do the journey and the Universe will have your back. Even when it seems She has abandoned you, She has not and will not do so. She is always there. And yes, I call her 'She' because She is the creator of all. It is the feminine who creates and yes, too, sometimes destroys.

You will only access Divine Joy when you are on the path to your Self. You may not even realise that you have made progress until you catch a glimpse of that feeling. It may arrive and depart swiftly, or not. But it is a sign you are on the right road. Enjoy the moments it gifts you, then continue on your path to Self.

It is a lifelong journey and it is what you are here in this human form to do. Anything else, is mere gravy, an accompaniment for the main meal.

That is all.

Do nothing

There is something to be said for lying around in the sun and doing nothing. But most of you have forgotten how to do this simplest of human tasks – to do nothing.

When did you lose it? Who can tell. Was it around the time the powers-that-be told you that you must work, work, work to have value?

They were wrong.

What is worse though, much, much worse, is that by forgetting how to do nothing, you often lose your ability to create something. You have so much creativity inside you but, if you never give yourself time to rest and just be, that creativity screams with anguish and after a while, dies a horrible and traumatic death.

Your creativity wants to flow through you every day, day in, day out. But if you are never still or allowing yourself the wilful pleasure of staring into the middle distance at nothing and allowing yourself to daydream, well, creativity doesn't really get a look in.

Yes, yes, creativity can flourish under pressure in some circumstances. But the creativity that flourishes at other times is just as, or perhaps even more, valuable because it does not require you to produce it just because you're supposed to.

Think of the last time you were immersed in a creative activity. Perhaps you were painting, cooking, writing or building something. Whatever it was, consider those moments when you were fully present to what you were doing. Your creativity flowed through your Soul and out your fingertips or toes or mouth, effortlessly, like wine from a bottle. It. Just. Flowed.

There is a message for you in that.

Creativity is not really a cerebral exercise although many would no doubt argue that point and yes, they are welcome to their opinions, tenfold. I am not interested in arguing the point.

But consider this: When you feel called to create something, that desire comes from deep within. It doesn't come from outside although yes, perhaps you may see or hear something that sparks the inspiration for your creative endeavour. But the actual creative act is drawn from deep within you and is wholly and solely yours. What a miracle!

Yet, many do not value it enough. People consider doing nothing as wasteful or, even worse, non-productive. Let me tell you something: If you humans don't stop running around like crazy dervishes then your nervous systems will simply pack it in and your human fleshy casing and innards will also suffer.

Creativity is nourishment not just for your Soul but also for your mind, your emotional body, your physical body and your energetic body. It helps you line everything up the way nature intended. Yes, nature loves the creative force. When was that important fact lost in the annals of history?

All I ask is that you consider the burden you carry when you don't harness and explore your creativity, and the burden you will release when you do.

When you create, you become lighter energetically. It is clarifying. Think of it like a filter for dirty water. It clears everything. You will think more clearly afterwards and even better will be that feeling of satisfaction that you created something of your own. Your hands, your Soul, your fingertips, or perhaps your feet or mouth or arms, created something. And there is always, always magic in that thing you create.

Creativity is magic. It is magic in plain sight.

Don't let the naysayers fool you. You all have magic within you and you can access it anytime you choose. You just need to open up the portals of your Soul with nothing...doing nothing... allowing space to do nothing.

Oh, how I wish you would daydream more. Instead of snapping that little child's attention back into the room when they gaze at nothing, let them gaze a little longer, then push some paper, pens, paints, clay or something else under their nose and see what happens.

You see, you don't have to think to create. You just need to flow. It is those moments between conscious thoughts where the creativity peeks through and for a moment, just a moment, it calls forth the question, "What if?"

Magic will invariably follow.

Of course, you may hate what you create. Despise it. Others may too. All those critical minds, including yours, saying your creation is not good enough, cutting-edge enough, complex enough. Worse still, they might say it is naïve and not well thought through. How terrible indeed to be accused of creating from a place where pre-existing knowledge is abandoned. Not.

If you take one precious thought from all of this, one piece of guidance to move forward with, please make it this: Create.

Make time to unravel the convolutions of your mighty mind by allowing it to still with nothingness. Allow the daydreams, the non-productivity, the time-wasting. Allow them into your life regularly and frequently. Schedule them if you must, but allow them most definitely.

Allow yourself to be free from the musts and the to-dos and the shoulds. Then just wait and see what creativity flows.

Love 1

I want to talk to you about love. Love in a way that most of you have no clue about. I would say, when it comes to love, most of you are looking the wrong way and frequently being hit by the proverbial bus as a result.

Love is divine. Love is kind. Love is compassionate. And, above all, love has boundaries.

The number of you who are yet to learn this great, great lesson, is diabolically huge. Seriously, you have been misled about what love is.

Yes, there are many different types of love – the love of a parent for a child, the love of a woman for a man, the love of a woman for another woman and so on. There are many different types but they all have one thing in common if they are done right: They do not and never will involve you deliberately hurting the person you love. Because love is not about pain. It is not about inflicting pain. It just isn't.

Yes, sometimes you will accidentally hurt the person you love. Perhaps your shadows and insecurities will come out to play as you reflect each other's traumas and lessons. But to deliberately hurt someone you love, is not love. It is viciousness. Worse still, is when you deliberately hurt the person you claim to love, and then when they object (which of course, they will, who wouldn't), you say it is their fault and they made you do it. Or you will issue the classic non-apology, saying, "I'm sorry you feel that way" as you continue to take zero responsibility for your own hurtful behaviour and continue to have zero intentions of changing it.

That is not love.

It is not.

The story you are all fed about love equalling pain is absolutely appalling and singularly unhelpful when you are trying to work out what love is and how to express it.

How did it all get so screwed up? Well, yes, you could look at the things you watch on screens or perhaps even the books you have read, but the answer lies much more deeply than that. It lies in the fabric of your societies and the families you are born into, along with the generational traumas your parents, aunts, uncles, brothers, sisters, cousins and beyond bring forward with them in their cellular memory.

I tell you: Love is not pain. It never was.

Yes, you may love and not have it returned and that will feel painful. It will hurt as you process any feelings of rejection and so on that you may feel. You will feel the loss of someone you regarded as precious. That is part of the growth of your Soul in this lifetime, to feel these things. Sometimes the feelings may almost carry you away. Some have indeed checked out completely with the grief of losing someone they held dear. Doctors talk of people dying from heartbreak. So yes, there is pain in loss of love.

But love itself is never about inflicting pain. And this is where you can become unstuck if that is all you know and you have become accustomed to believe it is normal.

If your parents deliberately hurt you through their actions, words or their neglect, that was not an expression of their love towards you. How then do you know what love is or feels like if you have not experienced it from those who society says must love you the most, and are obligated through family ties to love you?

The short answer is: It is incredibly and excruciatingly difficult for you to know. Your nervous system becomes acclimatised to the trauma of pain equalling love and your mind believes things must be a certain way to receive a skerrick of love and so your journey into pain begins. But this pain is not love. It is just pain.

The continuing belief and social narrative that family is the source of security and love is false. Yes, your conditioning throughout evolution has brought you to this point, brought all humans to this point, and much of that has been through staying close to the family unit no matter how poorly they treated you. After all, when faced with other tribes or those who wished to kill you, a group of people bound together with blood ties was your best chance of survival.

But you are no longer in that place in time. You are no longer there. You are here and you must recognise and understand that oftentimes the family unit is your biggest teacher of what love isn't, rather than what love is.

It is hard to break these ties and the patterns that hold onto us when it comes to love. You go from a family and upbringing where love looked like one thing (an unhealthy thing) and you set off to create love as an adult, often not realising that the love you are seeking to replicate is not good for you. It is toxic. Like drinking arsenic voluntarily, you chug it down and for some, very sadly, it may even kill you emotionally, spiritually or physically.

If this is the time for love to rise then I ask for only one thing from you: Understand that where you've come from and all those patterns you learned may no longer serve you, and you must leave them behind if you wish to thrive in this ever-evolving world.

Love is not pain. Love has boundaries. Love lifts you. That is what love is.

Think less

I want to ask you to think less. Much less. I appreciate this will be difficult for most of you. But I want you to turn your attention to your thoughts and recognise just how much they are ruling your life. Seriously, do you realise how much they constrict and take you away from the truth of your journey here on this planet, right now? It really is madness; an affliction almost all suffer from relentlessly.

You may think my advice is given glibly. How can you 'think' less? You're doing the best you can to manage everything, and anxiety is natural and so many people have it and, and, and...

Stop.

You must learn to feel more than you think. Your mind is not the future driver as we have discussed elsewhere. You must feel and process what you feel. Then make your decisions from there.

Actually, no. This may be where you become confused. Let me clarify. There are two different types of senses I am referring to here – the feeling of your emotions as they course through your body at all hours, minutes and seconds of the day and night, and your intuitive feelings.

You must learn to understand the former in order to tune in effectively to the latter.

Your intuition is your greatest guide but it is too frequently drowned out by those other feelings you have - the feelings that too often originate in the mind. Damn that mind with its own agenda to control, conform and do what it believes is needed to survive. Sometimes yes, the mind is right. But if you wish to evolve and walk more easily through this changing world, and understand yourself more and your place in the world too, you must have a serious conversation with your mind and then choose a different way to be.

Feelings are just feelings. They will hurt, exhilarate or bring you to your knees. This is true. But in essence they are only feelings and they eventually move on to be replaced by more feelings – feelings usually generated by thoughts.

Your intuition, and the feelings and knowing it evokes, is not guided or infiltrated by the mind. Your intuition has another agenda entirely. Your intuition, your gut instinct, is by far the most important tool you have at your disposal to help keep you safe, expand, live in alignment and feel more calm than your mind has ever allowed you to be.

But to tune into your intuition, you must manage the feelings generated by the mind. Otherwise, your inner voice, because it frequently speaks quietly, will be drowned out, ignored or mistranslated.

I want you to practise using your intuition now, more than ever. Learn how to manage the incessant mutterings of your mind and the feelings it creates.

I am not speaking of detachment from self here. No. I am not here for that because you are human and here to feel. Most of you are not built to sit upon a mountain top, or hide in a cloister in silence, praying for change and kindness. A very few of you maybe, but most of you are not.

So, yes, you are here to feel your emotions and travel the journey of feeling all the emotions humans are built to feel. That is the way it should be.

But. But. It is important to find ways to silence that mind occasionally or, at least, reduce its raucous roars to a quieter murmur. Otherwise it will be almost impossible for your intuition to get a word in edgewise. Ha! Your mind will be happy with that state of affairs but your Soul will not be.

Think less. Find ways to be present more. Allow your feelings to be felt, then release them through your toes. Scream your grief into the atmosphere. Feel it all, the pain, the joy, the everything.

Then find your way back to the pockets of silence within. Cultivate them. Know there is no right or wrong way to do this. Know only that it is important you do this, so you can live an intuitive lifestyle.

What you're not noticing

There is a lot of talk about division and indeed a lot of division is happening. Stress and trauma makes people divide and congregate then divide again. Times are tough.

But when you talk of some great figure pulling the strings from an unknown location, the cabals and the elite, you blame them for your state of affairs. You blame them for the pain and the division.

You blame them when you should blame yourself.

I realise this is a bitter pill to swallow but just as there is no white knight coming on a horse to rescue you, there is no dark knight hiding around the corner to pillory you or hoist your head upon a petard.

Aren't you tired of blaming something else instead of dealing with what you have been dealt? Truthfully, aren't you exhausted from pushing away your own responsibility for the state of the world?

In the *Wizard of Oz*, the man who was most feared was a small man who hid behind a large curtain and an even larger machine. He was not fearsome but he was himself, full of fear. What does that tell you about the predicament humans find themselves in?

Yes, there are people in the world who operate more from their shadows than their light. And yes, they create pain for others wilfully and often with no compunction, compassion or gratitude. But make no mistake, those people have flourished, grown and gained their power because of you.

Every time you looked the other way. You.

Every time you voted for someone who told you what you wanted to hear, even though you knew he did not treat others so well. You.

Every time you went to a rally and marched alongside someone who previously espoused beliefs you hate, but now they believe in your cause, so march on, you do. You.

Every time you laughed at someone's cruelty or said it's not your problem because the ones who were treated cruelly were not you. You.

Every time you watched someone's pain on screen for entertainment and paid money for it. You.

Weeds do not grow unless we wilfully ignore them and wilfully refuse to pull them out by the roots.

You.

What you're not seeing is you. You in everything you rage against. You the divisive one. You the one screaming your rights at another. You.

You helped create this world. You are a participant. Own your role in it.

It is not enough to point the fingers and say, "They don't agree with me and therefore they are wrong".

You.

What you're not seeing is the ones who are trailing behind you. Other people are watching and following you. You're not noticing the ones standing beside you - the ones who are happy to gain your confidence and tell you a similar story to yours, just for now, because it is convenient.

What you're not noticing, is that you're the one doing the dividing. Humans are doing the dividing. There is no need for some great anonymous power or a group of secretive individuals to exist for the division to happen.

You are the division.

Stop pointing out there and saying, "Them! It is them who are the problem".

It's not them. It's you.

But you are only a 'problem' until you choose to own your role.

Make different choices at the ballot box. Make different choices in how you spend your money, where you live and how you interact with the world.

The one thing you can change is you. The problem is not out there, it is within you.

You have capacity to choose rightness over convenience. What will you sacrifice to change the world? Pointing way, way out there and blaming them is a waste of time when the real problems are here, on your street, in your town and in your life.

What you're not noticing is there is no great divisive power calling the shots and driving you against each other. There is only a bunch of humans, like millions of ants crawling on the surface of this planet, trying to dominate others and assert their rights but not let go of anything in the process. You must release many things. You must make different choices. You are the powerhouse in your life, on this planet.

Will you choose inconvenience and stay in the light? Or choose to blame others for the predicaments you all had a role in creating and perpetuating?

It is convenient to blame 'out there' for the pain. And yes, there is a lot of pain. But there cannot be Great Change without Great Discomfort and you cannot avoid your own responsibility for the way things are or the way things can be.

Move from your heart, not your head. Move with grace. Stop blaming others. Look in your homes at your own choices. Look at what your neighbours are doing.

Begin choosing more inconvenience and discomfort because you know in your heart and Soul that you have a role to play in this Great Change.

Choose wisely. Forget the narratives of division.

Choose wisely. Choose to be more than you have ever been before.

Love 2

In your relationships with other humans there is one fundamental truth that binds you — you are all fundamentally the same and there is nothing within them that is also not within you.

You may look at a murderer, a sociopath and recoil saying, "No, I could never be like that!". But I promise you, given the right circumstances, the right experiences (or perhaps, the worst possible experiences), you could be that person too.

The majority of people on the planet were not born murderers or sociopaths devoid of the higher and kinder emotions associated with the human experience. Some have become that way out of necessity and in response to what life has thrown at them, even, sometimes, from before birth. Even in the womb they were absorbing from their mother and her environment the way of things.

While there are a few, certainly, who will never be able to access the higher vibration emotions of love and empathy, most have felt them at one point and may still feel them for some people, while inflicting pain on others.

Disturbing though this is, it is the way of things and it is best to be honest with yourselves about how humankind and the individuals within your species have arrived at this place, and where future interventions are needed to walk back some of the damage that has been inflicted on innocent infants who then become not-so-innocent children, teens and adults.

We could talk of the psychology of it all, how the brain changes with exposure to the toxic and unhealthy, of nature and nurture. But that is not what I wish to focus on and also, to be frank, it probably won't help you now as you cannot undo what has already been done to yourself or others – you can only grow and expand and hopefully, if you step into your role of personal and communal responsibility, take actions to prevent such damages occurring to those who have just arrived on your planet or who are yet to arrive.

Investment is required now, not later, now, in the kind of world you wish to create for the young and future generations, and for yourselves now.

It must be an investment of love. Love even when you want to turn away, reject, pull away, put down, run away, ostracise, disappear, disorganise, repudiate, rage against or disparage.

Love.

What do I mean exactly?

What I mean is this: In times of turbulence, disorganisation and upheaval, it will be common and has always been common to turn on each other, form tribal alliances and fight with those who do not agree with your way. This is a safety response to threats (real or imagined) and resistance to changing the ways you have grown comfortable with.

Just because your ways are comfortable, does not mean they serve the highest good of others, of the planet, or even ultimately, you.

You know this is a time of change and disruption, and part of that disruption is a calling to love when it would be easier to hate, to include when it would be easier to ostracise, and to be compassionate when it would be easier to be harsh.

How difficult is it to love those who would scream into your face with all their might that you are wrong and they are right?

It is very hard. For the most part, it is very hard indeed. And forgive me, but I am not for one single moment saying you should ever tolerate abuse in any form directed at you. That is not love for self if you do – and love must be for self as well as for others. It cannot only be about them because that is martyrdom and victimhood and you are not here for that.

So, it is love with boundaries and the seeking of good in others that is needed.

It can be extraordinarily difficult in these times to keep looking for the good when you see so much wrong. So many people are being carried away by fear right now. They believe it is their intuition but it is not. It is their fears. They turn away from the media they don't wish to see in the hope that will protect them. But it won't. You cannot turn away or run from something forever, not when you are part of the ecosystem in which it was created. Denial of the existence of one thing does not make it disappear or not exist. It still exists, you're just pretending it doesn't.

I understand it is hard, but if you keep turning from reality - the reality all humans are faced with - nothing will really change much at all. You will all just hurtle towards the abyss much faster. That is the way of things.

There is a saying, "You cannot run from yourself because you are always with yourself".

You cannot run from you, and when you fully understand there is nothing in another that does not also reside in you, it may be hugely clarifying and empowering for some, but debilitating and distressing for others.

How do you make peace with the fact that you are the same as those you despise?

You don't. Most of you will resist this with all your might. Fighting, fighting, fighting it.

"I mustn't get angry. I must be nice. I must be tolerant. I must take the higher ground."

You are fighting your most basic and instinctual nature when you embark on that road without acknowledging there is a very large part of you that has the capacity to, and would very much like to, take the so-called 'lower' road inside you.

Is it really lower to get angry and express your discontent?

No.

Is it really so bad to not be tolerant or not nice?

No.

It is not bad to be these things or feel these things. But it isn't socially acceptable and therein lies the issue.

Social acceptability is the issue.

"What am I if my actions are not socially acceptable?" you ask. "Nothing," is the answer you believe.

I'm not so sure about that.

I am not suggesting you be cruel, malicious or deliberately unkind or worse. I am suggesting you accept and see that you have those parts in you, as much as anyone else has them too.

You are no different, no better and no worse. You just make a different choice, right now in this moment, to someone else's choice.

Life is a series of choices – this saying is trite, but true all the same.

Your choices may take you where you want to go. Sometimes they will take you in a direction you do not want to go, yet you made all the choices that led you to that point so you must own that too.

This does not, by any means, suggest or imply that you are responsible for any abuse inflicted upon you by another. That is their responsibility and their choice, never yours.

But rather, your choice in any given moment will take you in a certain direction and that is what you are responsible for. I hope you can discern the difference in this point.

Humans would be much better served by accepting all their shadows, looking honestly at them and knowing them for what they are – a part of their complexity as humans – rather than seeking to only and always dance in the light.

There is light and shadow in all things and there is absolutely light and shadow in you.

If you can accept this, it positions you to better understand the actions of those you despise and would never wish to be aligned with in your views or actions. Although, I am not for one minute suggesting that you do align with them.

But, I am suggesting, recommending, philosophising even, that until you recognise that they are the same as you, just shaped by different experiences but holding the same capacities within them – they just make different choices about which capacities they choose to spend more of their time within – the better it will be for all of you.

Stop turning away from those you don't want to listen to, from those who say things you don't want to hear. It won't make them go away and it won't protect you either. It simply won't.

Understand, instead, that they are showing you parts of you that you wish to avoid. Be honest and own these parts. You don't have to dance with them in your life, but just see them for what they are – they are part of you. Then you can begin to move more fully towards love for self, and a greater and more defined love for others.

Love 3

Life is never going to be perfect. I know you don't want to hear that, but it won't be. There is no Utopia for humanity. There never was, nor will there ever be.

Does this thought depress you? Do you hope for more?

If so, may I enquire, why? What more do you seek that you do not already have within you to give and to receive?

Ah, the practicalities of life. Are you concerned with only your practicalities or the practicalities of others?

What would you do with that million dollars you dream of? Invest it wisely? Blow it all within a few years? Donate it?

Do you realise that even if you did all of that, you would still not have anything that feels like perfection? That is what Utopia is, 'perfection', where everything is always right and calm, peaceful and good.

Stop, I beg you. Stop thinking of Utopia because it simply does not and never will marry up with the human experience.

Perfection does not exist in nature so why do you believe it could exist in humankind or in the societies you create?

Even if every star aligned, all war and poverty ended, everyone had enough to eat and there was no further abuse of anyone, would there be a Utopia then? Would every single person on the planet be satisfied then?

It seems unlikely, does it not?

Stop aiming for Utopia. Instead, look at what you have and make it better. Love what you have right now, in this moment, and make it better. No, I most definitely do not mean make it better at the expense of another. Obviously, not that.

I mean make the world better. Set that as your intent every single day: "How can I make the world a better place today?" Ask yourself this question regularly and with intention. Then do what comes up for you.

Perhaps the answer is, smile and say hello to every person you meet. Perhaps it is a far more grandiose gesture. It matters not what you do, only that your intention is clear.

How can you make the world a better place?

Love, showing love, being more aligned with love, is the key to it all.

Will it create Utopia? No. Not in a thousand years. Humans are simply not there yet.

But coming at the world from a clear intention of, "How can I make the world a better place today, a better place for others to live in?" – now that is something that can change everything.

You all have a role to play, every single one of you, in making this spinning rock you inhabit, a better place.

Some of you will spend a lot of time avoiding that role. Others may never inhabit it. Others will tell themselves they are making things better when really, they are only nurturing their ego rather than the true needs of humankind.

This is the complexity of your experiences and your journeys.

Calls for Utopia are greatly over-rating that experience. Most of you would find it extraordinarily dull and tedious if everything always went your way all the time. You would become increasingly spoilt and despotic if this occurred. And we have enough spoilt and despotic humans on the planet already, thank you very much.

So, no. There is no Utopia. But there doesn't need to be.

There does need to be love, and lots of it.

Your love for self and love for others can move mountains and create miracles in places where others only see bricks and impenetrable walls. That is what love does – it finds and shows the way forward when the odds are seemingly insurmountable.

Love is the most powerful driver of the human experience and of human actions and interactions with each other.

Think on this: If you loved yourself deeply, what would you do differently today or even in this moment? Ah, I know so many things are running through your mind right now. Are you going to do any of them?

Now, next question: If you loved others deeply, even strangers, what would you do differently today or even in this moment? Not selective love. It must be deliberate and chosen love. What would you do then?

Some of you may find one of these questions more difficult than the other. Some of you will find both challenging. Others may throw their hands up in disgust and say, at least in their minds, "This is ridiculous! This whole love thing is a waste of time and changes nothing, so why even bother?"

If you are in this last group, I understand why you feel this way. Truly, I do. In a world so cruel and misaligned with real and deliberately-chosen love, it can be easy to become so distanced from it, that it is almost unrecognisable to you. I get it.

But. But. But. Love is the only thing that will save you in the end and everything will grow from that. It just will.

It may feel uncomfortable because it is so foreign. It may feel wasteful because you don't see many other people doing it.

It may feel like a poor choice when there are so many other important things to do (in your mind, at least, they are more important).

Calm. Calm your busy mind for a moment. Then a moment more, and a moment more after that. Breathe, in and out, and in and out. Slow yourself down completely to this breath, then this one, then the next.

Then ask yourself two questions:

"How can I deliberately choose and demonstrate my love for myself today?"

"How can I deliberately choose and demonstrate my love for others today?"

Ask yourself both these questions and I promise you, the right answers will come.

The answers and the actions you take will not lead to any Utopia wrapped in fictional narratives of fantasy, and distracted, hopeful desire. No. They will not do that.

But they will take you somewhere else entirely. And I promise you, the world will slowly, little by little, become a better world for you and everyone else as a result.

Love will change it all. Humans just need to begin choosing it today, tomorrow, the next day and the day after that.

Author's note

Dear Reader,

For whatever reason, the Universe decided I was the right person to bring through the messages contained in this book. The words arrived swiftly and the entire work was completed within a few short weeks.

After I brought through each chapter, I would revisit my words, wondering if they would make sense. Surprisingly, they always did. That is the constant adventure of channelled writing - you never know what is coming through your fingertips and onto the page, until after it has arrived.

Like many people, I often feel concerned about the world we are creating and our future. Perhaps you feel the same. I hope for better days and this book reminds me that, working together, we can create them. We all have choices to make and actions to take, or not.

It really is in our hands. It is in your hands.

It is time to start.

Lots of love,
Lucretia x

PS. If you would like to stay in touch, please join my Lucretia's Letters mailing list at
http://eepurl.com/imGzcw

About the author

Lucretia is a multi-passionate creative who believes we all have the power to make the world a better place. Her work as an author, strategist, intuitive and transformational teacher, advocate and psychic channel focuses on healthy relationships, sensitivity and alignment to purpose.

Lucretia explores healthy love on her YouTube channel, Dear Lucretia, and empowers everyday people to stop sexual violence through her enterprise, the Stop Sexual Violence Collaboration and the associated podcast, Medusa's Mic.

An Intuitive Lifestyle is Lucretia's second book. Her previous work, *The Men I've Almost Dated*, is a voyeuristic, thoughtful and sometimes mortifying memoir about a woman who is determined to follow her heart wherever it leads, even when the road is a dead end.

Lucretia dreams of moving to Italy to establish a creative school for sensitive souls.

www.ingramcontent.com/pod-product-compliance
Lightning Source LLC
Chambersburg PA
CBHW050447010526
44118CB00013B/1712